Muscle Cars

Katharine Bailey

x1000r/min

CRABTREE PUBLISHING COMPANY
www.crabtreebooks.com

Crabtree Publishing Company
www.crabtreebooks.com

To my dad, Paul Bailey, for sharing his knowledge and lifelong love of muscle cars.

Coordinating editor: Ellen Rodger
Series and project editor: Rachel Eagen
Editors: Carrie Gleason, Adrianna Morganelli, L. Michelle Nielsen
Design and production coordinator: Rosie Gowsell
Production assistance: Samara Parent
Art direction: Rob MacGregor
Scanning technician: Arlene Arch-Wilson
Photo research: Allison Napier

Consultant: Andrew Elliot

Photo Credits: PhotoSpin, Inc/Alamy: p. 1; Phil Talbot/Alamy: p. 12 (both); Transtock Inc./Alamy: p. 7 (top); Jim West/Alamy: p. 28 (top), p. 29 (bottom); Bettmann/Corbis: p. 16 (top), p. 19 (bottom), p. 30; Rainer Holz/zefa/Corbis: p. 5 (top); Charles O'Rear/Corbis: p. 17 (bottom); Neil Rabinowitz/Corbis: p. 10; Roger Ressmeyer/Corbis: p. 31 (top); John Springer Collection/Corbis: p. 14 (top);

Courtesy of the Detroit News: p. 11 (bottom); Ron Kimball/Ron Kimball Stock: cover, p. 4 (both), p. 5 (bottom), p. 6, p. 7 (bottom), p. 8, p. 11 (top), p. 13 (both), p. 14 (bottom), p. 15 (both), p. 16 (bottom), p. 17 (top), p. 18 (both), p.19 (top), p. 20, p. 21 (both), p. 23 (both), p. 24 (both), p. 25 (both), p. 26, p. 27 (both), p. 28 (bottom), p. 29 (top); Motorsports Images & Archives Photography. Used with permission: p. 31 (bottom); Randolph King/Photo Researchers, Inc.: p. 22

Illustrations: Dan Pressman: p. 9

Cover: Dodge created some of the most memorable muscle cars, including this 1971 Dodge Challenger.

Title page: Powerful engines and high speeds were the name of the game during the muscle car era.

Library and Archives Canada Cataloguing in Publication

Bailey, Katharine, 1980-
  Muscle cars / Katharine Bailey.
(Automania!)
Includes index.
ISBN-13: 978-0-7787-3010-1 (bound)
ISBN-10: 0-7787-3010-7 (bound)
ISBN-13: 978-0-7787-3032-3 (pbk.)
ISBN-10: 0-7787-3032-8 (pbk.)

    1. Muscle cars--Juvenile literature. 2. Muscle cars--United States--Juvenile literature. I. Title. II. Series.

TL23.B33 2006   j629.222   C2006-902462-6

Library of Congress Cataloging-in-Publication Data

Bailey, Katharine, 1980-
  Muscle cars / written by Katharine Bailey.
    p. cm. -- (Automania!)
  Includes index.
  ISBN-13: 978-0-7787-3010-1 (rlb)
  ISBN-10: 0-7787-3010-7 (rlb)
  ISBN-13: 978-0-7787-3032-3 (pbk)
  ISBN-10: 0-7787-3032-8 (pbk)
  1. Muscle cars--United States--Juvenile literature. I. Title. II. Series.
  TL23.B256 2006
  629.222--dc22

                    2006014364

Crabtree Publishing Company

www.crabtreebooks.com   1-800-387-7650

Published in Canada
Crabtree Publishing
616 Welland Ave.
St. Catharines, ON
L2M 5V6

Published in the United States
Crabtree Publishing
PMB16A
350 Fifth Ave., Suite 3308
New York, NY 10118

Published in the United Kingdom
Crabtree Publishing
White Cross Mills
High Town, Lancaster
LA1 4XS

Published in Australia
Crabtree Publishing
386 Mt. Alexander Rd.
Ascot Vale (Melbourne)
VIC 3032

Contents

Metal Meets Muscle

Muscle cars are flashy, powerful cars built for speed. The first muscle cars were built in 1964, and they remained popular until 1971. Muscle cars ruled the streets with their roaring engines, bright paint colors, and high-speed performance.

Super Cars with Style

A muscle car is a two-door, mid-sized **coupe** with a large, powerful engine. At the height of the muscle car era, these cars featured flashy paint colors, bold racing stripes, and special brand badges, which are metal or plastic logos that are applied to the exteriors of cars. Muscle cars also had cool wheels, eye-catching **grilles**, and hood scoops. A hood scoop is an air vent in the hood of a car. It is designed to bring cooler outside air into the engine compartment to make the engine perform better. Some hood scoops are non-functional, and are only for decoration.

Many muscle cars are valuable collectors items, such as this Oldsmobile 4-4-2. Most were originally sold at dealerships for less than $5,000, but are worth more today.

Built to Drive

Muscle cars were first used for racing, but they became popular for regular street driving as well. In the 1960s, a popular weekend activity for young people was watching drag races at favorite local racing spots, such as unused airport landing strips or quiet stretches of road. A drag race is a competition in which two cars race down a quarter-mile stretch. Muscle cars were built to be driven at high speeds and usually did not have luxuries, such as carpeting or heaters. These items would have made passengers more comfortable, but also added weight and made the cars slower.

American Muscle

American car companies General Motors (GM), Ford, and Chrysler competed to build the best muscle cars with the most powerful engines. GM released muscle cars under several of its **divisions,** including Buick, Chevrolet, Oldsmobile, and Pontiac. Ford made popular models under its own name, and under the **brand name** Mercury. Chrysler created muscle cars in two of its divisions, Dodge and Plymouth. A smaller company, American Motors Corporation (AMC), also made muscle cars.

(above) Two drivers speed down a stretch of road in a dangerous drag race.

(right) This modern car displays its Hemi engine, an engine that defined the muscle car era.

Options

Muscle cars were sold as option packages. An option package includes extra features that are added to a base model, or the original version of a car that is made in a factory. During the muscle car era, option packages included high-performance engines, special badges or racing stripes, and **sport suspensions**. Option packages allowed people to **upgrade** their cars at extra cost.

The Stage is Set

Muscle cars brought the look of racing to the street. Before the mid-1960s, only expensive luxury cars or sports cars had high-performance engines. The Chrysler C-300 changed this, creating a car that could perform like a race car but also be used as a passenger vehicle.

The Hemi Takes Charge

The Chrysler C-300, first built in 1955, is often called the forefather of muscle cars. It is not considered a true muscle car because it was large and expensive, while real muscle cars were mid-sized and less luxurious. The C-300 had Chrysler's famous Hemi engine. The Hemi is a high-performance engine that was built for speed, and it was the most powerful engine used in a regular, factory-produced passenger car at this time. The C-300 included racing features such as dual exhaust pipes, special racing tires, and a lack of outside rear-view mirrors for a sleeker look.

Chevrolet Impala SS

The Chevrolet Impala of 1961 was another early muscle car. The base model came with the Super Sport, or SS, option package, which gave the car a sportier look. The SS option package included tri-blade spinners on the wheels, which were small metal blades in the middle of the wheel that spun like propellers. It also had a padded dashboard, like race cars at this time. The option package transformed the Impala into a race-ready vehicle, and it was a popular choice among American racing enthusiasts.

The C-300 was popular because it performed like a race car, and had the luxuries and handling of a passenger car.

6

(left) The Impala Super Sport option package featured special badges on the car body.

Ford Thunderbolt

The 1964 Ford Thunderbolt was an early drag-strip racer. It was a highly **modified** version of the popular Ford Fairlane. It broke speed records with its powerful engine and lightweight body. The Thunderbolt had the basic Fairlane design, but parts of its body were made of **fiberglass** rather than steel, including the hood, front fenders and bumper, and doors. Its side windows were made with **Plexiglas** rather than with regular glass. Only 100 Thunderbolts were ever produced. Its special design was expensive to make and its powerful engine and sport suspension made it impractical for everyday driving.

(below) The Ford Fairlane did not perform like the Thunderbolt, but it had the exterior stylings of a muscle car. It influenced other designs of the muscle car era.

Start Me Up!

Most cars are powered by internal combustion engines. In muscle cars, these engines usually have eight cylinders, which are arranged in a V-formation. This setup is called a V8.

Heart of the Machine

Internal combustion engines produce power by converting gasoline and air into energy. The V8 engine is an efficient design because it can produce a lot of power without taking up too much space. This allows the car to have a lower, flatter hood, making the car more **aerodynamic**.

The Hemi

A new version of the V8, the Hemi, was created by changing the shape of the combustion chamber heads at the top of the cylinders. Combustion chamber heads were usually flat, but on the Hemi, they were hemispherically shaped. The Hemi was a more efficient design, because it burned the air and gas mixture inside the chambers better. The hemispherical shape of the combustion chamber heads meant that less heat was lost. Hotter gases burn faster, and this is what gave the Hemi top performance.

(above right) This Hemi engine sits inside a 1971 Dodge Challenger. The efficient design made the Hemi the best engine for racing.

Horsepower

The term horsepower describes how much power an engine can produce, and is directly related to how much speed a car can achieve. The higher the horsepower rating, the faster a car can go. Regular cars were rated at around 150 horsepower, while muscle cars were usually rated at up to 500 horsepower or more.

spark plug

intake valve

exhaust valve

hemispherical cylinder head

piston

cylinder

connecting rod

crankshaft

Four-Stroke Cycle

This illustration shows how a Hemi engine works. Using the energy stored in gasoline, car engines create motion in four stages, known as the four-stroke cycle.

1. Intake

The piston, pulled downward in the cylinder by the connecting rod and turning crankshaft, draws air and fuel through the intake valve.

2. Compression

As the crankshaft spins, it moves the piston back up again. This **compresses** the air and gas mixture in the cylinder.

3. Power

When the piston reaches the top of the cylinder, the spark plug produces a tiny spark, combusting, or igniting, the air and gas. This creates a small explosion of energy, which drives the piston downward, and turns the crankshaft. The crankshaft completes its rotation, driving the piston back up.

4. Exhaust

As the piston comes up, the used combustion gases are forced through the exhaust valve. The gases exit the car through the exhaust pipe.

Engine Displacement

Engine displacement is the total volume of air and fuel mixture that an engine can pull into its combustion chamber during one cycle. The bigger an engine's displacement, the more power it can produce. Engine displacement is measured in units called cubic inches, or "c.i."

Dawn of the Age

The battle among manufacturers to create powerful engines fueled the public's desire for a street-ready racing machine. Pontiac met this desire by creating the affordable, speedy GTO.

The Legendary GTO

The Pontiac GTO is thought of as the car that kicked off the muscle car era. It featured all of the elements that would later define muscle cars, including an option package with a high-displacement engine and race-inspired accessories. Best of all, it was affordable for the average car buyer. The GTO was a wild success and the managers at General Motors set out to make more models in its other divisions.

Ready for Speed!

The GTO option package included a big block, or large sized, high-horsepower V8 engine. "Big block" is a term used to describe a high-displacement engine. The GTO package also came with GTO badges, tri-blade spinners, and single or dual hood scoops. A vacuum-operated exhaust (VOE) option was added to later models that allowed drivers to alter the flow of air out of the exhaust pipe by pulling a knob on the dashboard. This created a roaring sound when the car revved up.

The GTO was first built in 1964. The medium-sized coupe was made to appeal to young people. It offered high performance with an affordable price tag.

Oldsmobile Follows Pontiac

The success of the Pontiac GTO inspired other divisions of General Motors to produce their own muscle cars. One of their first models was the Oldsmobile 4-4-2. It debuted in 1964 with a high-displacement engine and sport suspension. It had special badges that said 4-4-2, which meant it had a four-barrel **carburetor**, four-speed gearbox, or transmission, and dual exhaust pipes. It also featured large racing tires, designed to give the car more stability when it launched from the starting line in a race, and more control on corners.

(below) The Oldsmobile 4-4-2 was respected as a race car, but it did not sell as well as the GTO on the street.

The Motor City

Detroit, Michigan, was the center of the muscle car universe. Many automotive factories and main offices were located in Detroit, and decisions about new models or rules regarding racing programs were said to "come from Detroit." Young people cruised up and down Woodward Avenue (below) to show off their cars. The street was also a favorite spot for street-racing in Detroit. The stoplights on Woodward Avenue became temporary starting gates on the weekends, as drivers revved up their engines and challenged other cars to stoplight-to-stoplight drag races.

Bigger is Better

The success of the Pontiac GTO prompted other car manufacturers to create their own race-ready coupes. This sparked a horsepower race, in which car companies competed with each other to produce top-performing engines.

A special version of the Dodge Charger was made for the popular television series, The Dukes of Hazzard. The car was called the General Lee.

Charged with Speed

One of the hottest muscle cars of 1966 was the Dodge Charger. It was fast and eye-catching, with an aerodynamic fastback roof. The fastback roof was a popular muscle car feature. The roof sloped down from the top of the car at an angle, almost reaching down to the tip of the trunk. The Charger featured what Dodge called an electric razor grille, which extended horizontally across the front of the car. The most impressive feature of the Charger was its engine, which was a detuned, or less powerful, version of the original Hemi. This was known as the street Hemi. This made it more practical for everyday driving.

Ford Fairlanes

In 1966, Ford added the GT and GTA option packages to its Fairlane 500 and 500XL models, and increased the engine compartment to accommodate a big block engine. The GT and GTA packages differed only in horsepower, the GTA having a more powerful engine. These packages included sport suspension and **disc brakes**, which helped slow down the cars from high speeds. The GT and GTA packages offered fiberglass hoods, as well as hood scoops to help the engines perform better. These option packages made the Fairlane a serious drag racer and were installed in only 60 cars.

(left) The Dodge Coronet R/T is a good example of how muscle cars appealed to race enthusiasts. The R/T stood for Road/Track, and the powerful Coronet was suited to both. It had a massive V8 engine. Beating the Coronet off the starting line was not easy!

(right) The Chevrolet Chevelle was a popular muscle car. In 1967, it was slightly redesigned to improve its handling with better tires and better brakes.

Heavy Duty Suspension

Most muscle cars were built with sport suspensions. The suspension is the system of springs and **shock absorbers** that help a car handle bumps in the road, slow down, and turn corners safely. Sport suspensions are stiffer than regular suspensions, and they were used in muscle cars to give drivers more control when they accelerated or braked suddenly, or took corners quickly. A sport suspension is required for race cars so they can handle properly, but the stiff springs can make for an uncomfortable ride because the driver and passengers feel every bump in the road.

More Than Muscle

The look of muscle cars was as important as their performance. The cars featured race-inspired details such as bold racing stripes, aerodynamic body design, and fancy wheels. Muscle cars stood out on the street and turned heads.

Soda Style

The muscle cars of the late 1960s had both power and style. Engines were as big as ever and car companies restyled existing models or debuted muscular new ones. The Dodge Charger was restyled in 1968 and kept a similar shape through to 1970. It was called the "Coke bottle" shape because from the side, it had the same curves as an old-fashioned glass Coke bottle. The problem with this design was that it was not very aerodynamic.

(above) A 1968 Charger leaps through the air during a chase scene from Bullitt, *a famous movie starring actor Steve McQueen.*

(above) Many muscle cars had few accessories to reduce weight and achieve even faster speeds, such as this 1964 Ford Thunderbolt.

Stripped Down

The original appeal of muscle cars was that they were fast and affordable. Many models were made even less expensive by keeping interior accessories to a minimum. A car such as the Plymouth Road Runner had rubber floor mats instead of carpeting. Other items common to most passenger cars that were usually removed on muscle cars included heaters, radios, and rearview mirrors. Muscle cars used on racetracks did not have these luxuries either.

Wild Colors

Chrysler introduced new paint colors for its muscle cars in the late 1960s. They were vibrant and unusual, with names like "Plum Crazy" purple, "Sublime" green, and "Banana Yellow." Unconventional colors were also used in cars' interiors. A black car might have yellow or red seats with matching floor mats.

(below) This 1970 Plymouth 'Cuda is painted in Plum Crazy.

The Road Runner

As time passed, muscle cars began featuring more accessories, which raised prices. In order to recapture the youth market that was unable to afford expensive cars, Plymouth debuted the Road Runner in 1968. It was an inexpensive muscle car with an impressive engine, just like the original Pontiac GTO. The Road Runner included a high-displacement engine with a ton of **torque**. The Road Runner name came from the Warner Bros. cartoon bird, and its horn made the same "beep beep!" sound as the character. The car also featured the Road Runner on its grille.

(below) The Road Runner came with an even more powerful engine option, which made it more expensive, but very fast. Its plain interior featured basic bench seats and few accessories.

Racing Fever

Car racing played a large role in how muscle cars were designed. Both professional and amateur car racing was popular in the 1960s and people wanted to experience the excitement of the racetrack on the streets.

(left) During a drag race in 1965, driver Richard Petty veered off of the track, accidentally killing a young boy.

Racing Series

Muscle cars were driven at official races hosted by racing organizations, such as the National Association of Stock Car Automotive Racing (NASCAR) and the National Hot Rod Association (NHRA). NASCAR races are held on oval-shaped tracks. NHRA races were quarter-mile drag races. Both the NASCAR and NHRA racing circuits were made for stock cars, or cars that had not been significantly modified from their original factory design. In order for cars to qualify as stock cars in the NASCAR or NHRA series, they had to fulfill requirements set by the organizations. This influenced the way muscle cars were designed and the engine options that became available to buyers.

(below) Pontiac offered a new version of the popular GTO in 1969. "The Judge" option package was inexpensive, fast, and flashy.

Making the Rules

In the 1950s, racing teams began modifying their cars more than ever. NASCAR's organizers realized that fewer cars on the track were coming straight from the factory. To change this, NASCAR ruled in 1965 that in order for a car to qualify as stock, at least 500 of its type of race engine had to be made available as options for buyers on cars sold at dealerships. The result was that sometimes more race models were made than could be sold. Race models were harder to drive because their stiff suspensions made them difficult to handle. They also lacked basic accessories and were more expensive to buy.

(top) The hood of the Mustang Boss 429 was made larger to fit its massive engine inside.

(right) A car burns rubber from its tires in a street race.

Breaking the Rules

Muscle cars were raced on tracks by professional drivers, but people also raced them on streets all across North America. Street racing was exciting for drivers and fans, but it was also very dangerous. Behind the wheels of powerful cars, drivers could easily lose control and cause accidents. This endangered the driver, other drivers on the road, as well as pedestrians. Street racing is now illegal and carries penalties, including **fines** or **confiscation** of the driver's car.

Stock Car Madness

The most outstanding cars of 1969 were ultra-aerodynamic stock cars. They looked unlike any other cars on the street and are still seen as some of the most outrageous vehicles ever designed.

Charging Ahead

In 1969, Dodge built two new Charger models. The Charger 500 had was more aerodynamic than the original Charger because of its sloped-down rear window and redesigned front end. The next version of the Charger, the Charger Daytona, was named after the Daytona 500 race in Florida. Unlike the boxier body shapes of traditional muscle cars, the Daytona was long and lean, featuring an extended, drooped-down nose and a massive spoiler. A spoiler is a metal bar across the back of the car that changes the flow of air around the car, which helps give the driver more control at high speeds. The Daytona was a successful NASCAR racer, but its race-specific design made it hard to sell in dealerships.

The Speedway Racer

The Ford Torino Talladega, built in 1969, was Ford's NASCAR racer. The Talladega was a speedier version of the Torino base model. Its race-ready features included a sloped-down nose for a more aerodynamic front and a fastback roof. The Talladega won a NASCAR Grand National Championship with driver David Pearson. Its successful racing record gave the car a reputation for high performance.

(above) The Charger Daytona was an excellent racer, but did not sell well off the racetrack. Only 500 Daytonas were ever made.

(left) The Mercury Cyclone GT, released from Ford in 1968, featured a fastback roof. The Cyclone was very popular.

A Mercury Storm

The 1969 Mercury Cyclone Spoiler II from Ford had an extended nose for better aerodynamics. Two styles of trim were available, named after two famous NASCAR drivers. The Dan Gurney edition featured a dark blue fastback roof, dark blue striping, and a decal, or label, of Gurney's name on the side. The Cale Yarborough edition had red striping and a decal of his signature.

(below) Due to giant spoilers, Superbirds and other Chryslers were called "Winged Warriors."

(bottom) NASCAR drivers (from left to right) Richard Petty, Cale Yarborough, and Lee Roy Yarborough pose in front of their cars at the Daytona 500 in 1968.

Plymouth Superbird

In 1970, NASCAR changed its rules about the minimum number of cars that manufacturers had to make available in dealerships. The new rule stated that car manufacturers had to make at least one unit for every dealership that sold a brand of car. For example, if 1,000 dealerships sold Plymouths, then 1,000 units of the same model had to be made. The 1970 Plymouth Superbird was one of the first stock cars made to follow this rule. Plymouth made 1,920 Superbirds. They were difficult to sell, because like the Daytona, they had an unusual body shape.

Bigger Than Ever

Some of the biggest engines of the muscle car era appeared in 1970. The cars were more powerful than ever, but the cost of insuring and fueling these gas-guzzlers made them expensive to own.

The Biggest on the Block

The most powerful cars of the muscle car era debuted in 1970. Two of the most impressive models were the Chevelle Super Sport 454 and the 1970 Buick Gran Sport 455. The new Chevy had a 454-cubic-inch engine, while the Buick had a 455-cubic-inch engine. Both cars roared off the starting line in races, and also handled well on the street. The Chevelle and the Gran Sport remain popular among muscle car enthusiasts, and rare, **restored** models can be seen on the streets today.

(below) The Chevrolet Chevelle Super Sport from 1970 had attractive striping, special SS badges, and a fastback roof.

Rebel with a Cause

The Rebel Machine, built in 1970, looked like an American flag with its red, white, and blue color scheme. It was the most powerful muscle car released from AMC. The Rebel Machine offered a fun, quick ride for recreational racers. It was not as powerful as some muscle cars at this time, but it could hold its own against several other models, including Chevrolet Chevelles and Ford Fairlanes. The Rebel Machine was also available in a black and silver paint scheme. The car included decals that read "The Machine" on either side. The Rebel Machine was made for only one year.

(above) This 1969 Hurst/Olds was fast and flashy, with gold stripes, functional hood scoops, and rear spoiler.

Pumped Full of Lead

Lead was first added to gasoline in the 1920s to help internal combustion engines perform better. Lead reduced engine knock, which is a chemical reaction that occurs in the combustion chambers of an engine. Muscle cars, which performed best with leaded gasoline, released **toxic emissions** into the air from their exhaust systems. Exposure to lead can cause blindness, cancer, or even death. In 1970, the United States government made changes to the **Clean Air Act** to phase out the use of leaded gasoline.

(below) The AMX from AMC debuted in 1968. It was not a true muscle car because it did not have back seats.

End of an Era

The muscle car era came to an end in 1971. A few new models appeared in the early 1970s, but concerns about air pollution and the availability of oil for gasoline meant the end of the classic American muscle car.

Cleaner Air

Muscle cars used much more gasoline than regular cars, because their engines were bigger and needed more fuel to get off the starting line quickly in a drag race. Changes to the Clean Air Act in 1970 required all car engines to have catalytic converters. Catalytic converters filter engine emissions so that fewer pollutants are released into the air.

(above) Gas-thirsty cars crowd a gas station in Brooklyn, New York, in 1973, despite signs explaining that the station was out of gas.

It's Going to Cost Ya

Automobile safety became an increasing concern in the early 1970s. Safety **spokespeople** began pointing out the dangers of driving fast, powerful vehicles. They felt that young people, who had little driving experience, should not be driving these vehicles because they were more likely to get into accidents. There were also concerns that the brakes on muscle cars did not work well enough to stop the cars safely, and that the tires were unsafe at high speeds. Insurance companies did not want to cover the costs of fixing damaged or wrecked muscle cars, so they discouraged people from driving them by raising the cost of insurance. Sales of muscle cars began to drop.

Oil Crisis

Concerns about the gasoline supply in 1973 further sealed the fate of muscle cars. That year, the Organization of the Petroleum Exporting Countries (OPEC) launched an oil **embargo** against the United States and other countries. Some countries in the **Middle East** wanted to punish the United States for supporting Israel in its war against Egypt. This caused the United States to get a much smaller amount of oil, which is needed to make gasoline, from the Middle East. The shortage caused gasoline prices in the United States to rise dramatically. Muscle cars quickly became unaffordable and impractical for many people.

(above) Beginning in 1970, carmakers began making cars with less powerful engines, but the Dodge Charger of 1971 was as powerful as ever. It featured a hood scoop that drivers activated by pressing a button on the dashboard.

Decline of American Muscle

The declining emphasis on power, due to the emission controls, meant that muscle cars of 1971 were more focused on appearance and accessories than they were on speed and power. This paved the way for a new generation of race-inspired cars. Pony cars and pocket rockets became the new weekend racers for car enthusiasts.

(below) The 1970 Buick GSX came in Saturn Yellow or Apollo White. Fewer than 700 GSXs were made that year.

Pony Up!

Pony cars are smaller versions of muscle cars. They debuted around the same time as muscle cars, but grew in popularity after 1971. Pony cars were fast, fun to drive, and more affordable than gas-thirsty muscle cars.

Small But Strong

(above) Barracudas had flat hoods, but 'Cudas had either functional or non-functional hood scoops. This hot pink 'Cuda has a functional hood scoop.

Pony cars had big, powerful engines in small, compact bodies. They usually featured four seats and had a sporty coupe design. They often came with racing features such as hood scoops, special badges, striping, and shiny, **chrome** wheels. Pony cars also had long hoods, short decks, or passenger areas, and short trunks. They were popular because they were still a race-style car, but did not have the high insurance costs, large size, or expensive price tags of high-performance muscle cars.

(left) The Ford Mustang Mach 1 had a shaker hood scoop, which included a device that sat at the top of the engine. It poked out of the hood to bring in outside air at high speeds.

The Mustang Is Born

The 1964 Ford Mustang started the pony car trend, but the model did not become popular until true muscle cars stopped being made. The first Mustangs were small and lightweight, but had the aggressive appearance of a classic muscle car. The Mustang was a huge hit. People loved that the Mustang was a flashy, fun, family car that could be modified into a weekend racer by purchasing the high-displacement engine option. The term "pony car" came from the horse logo that is featured on the grille of each Mustang.

(below) The Camaro was built to rival the Mustang and Barracuda. It had clean, curvy body lines and striping. The Z-28 option package included sport suspension, a high-horsepower engine, and racing stripes.

The Flashy Barracuda

Plymouth released a pony car in 1964 called the Barracuda. Its trademark was its slightly bubble-shaped glass back window that resembled a fishbowl. Plymouth advertised the Barracuda as a car that combined sporty performance with room for the family. It sat five people and had a roomy backseat and ample trunk space. Although the Barracuda was built to rival the Mustang, it was not nearly as popular and did not sell in numbers even close to Ford's pony car.

The Cool 'Cuda

In 1970, Plymouth released a flashier version of the Barracuda, called the 'Cuda. It arrived at the very end of the muscle car era, and was one of the last new models to offer high-performance engine options. The 'Cuda was one of the fastest drag racers of the muscle car era. It came in **hardtop** and convertible versions. The 'Cuda was not made in high numbers because public demand for high-powered engines had decreased. The Hemi engine was not offered as an option on the 'Cuda after 1970.

(below) The Plymouth Barracuda was redesigned for 1970 with a shorter body and a boxier trunk.

25

Pocket Rockets

Pocket rockets are inexpensive compact cars fitted with big, powerful racing engines for weekends at the drag strip. They became popular in the late 1960s. Young people with tight budgets could afford pocket rockets and the small, fast cars became a class of their own.

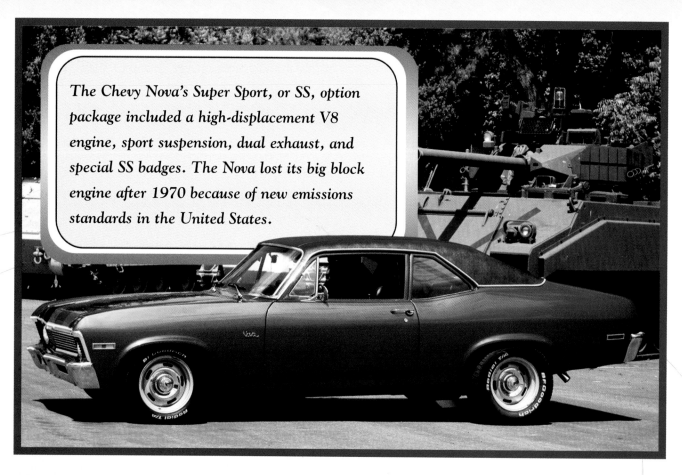

The Chevy Nova's Super Sport, or SS, option package included a high-displacement V8 engine, sport suspension, dual exhaust, and special SS badges. The Nova lost its big block engine after 1970 because of new emissions standards in the United States.

Little Rockets

Pocket rockets, also called compact cars, were smaller than regular muscle cars. They were less expensive to purchase than previous muscle cars, but they usually had powerful engines that allowed the cars to achieve high speeds. Pocket rockets appealed to young people because they were cheaper to insure and were less expensive to fuel than heavy muscle cars.

The Mighty Nova

The Chevy Nova of 1970 was a hit with drivers who wanted to drag race or cruise on the weekend but needed a reliable car for their weekday routine. The Nova was based on the Chevrolet Camaro platform, which means its basic body structure was the same as the Camaro. The Nova featured a Coke-bottle body shape and a race-inspired option package called the SS 396.

The Plymouth Duster had a powerful engine in a compact body.

Plymouth Duster

The 1970 Plymouth Duster was one of the hottest pocket rockets on the market. It was based on the Plymouth Valiant, a less expensive model in Plymouth's regular line of cars. The Duster appealed to young people who wanted a lot of horsepower for little cost. The Duster had several engine options, including the 340-cubic-inch V8. The Duster also included sport suspension, dual exhaust, and front disc brakes.

AMC AMX

The AMX debuted in 1968 and became one of AMC's most popular cars. It blended affordable pricing with distinctive design, and had enough horsepower to compete at weekend drag strips. The AMX came standard with a 290-cubic-inch V8 engine. As an option, buyers could upgrade to a 390-cubic-inch engine. Both engines packed a lot of horsepower. AMC's "Big Bad" option packages featured new colors such as "Big Bad Orange" or "Big Bad Green." The AMC AMX SS was built in limited numbers specifically for drag racing. The model is a rare find today and is valued as a collectible muscle car.

(below) The Dodge Dart was a popular pocket rocket. There were several different versions of the Dart, including the Dodge Demon, which appeared in 1971. The Demon 340 package featured a 340-cubic-inch V8 engine, dual hood scoops, and a rear spoiler.

Back in Black

Muscle cars made a comeback in the 1980s. Engines were built that met emissions standards while retaining their power and performance. In the early 2000s, new car models appeared, inspired by muscle car styles from the 1960s.

Technology Saves The Day

Improved technology and better design brought Detroit muscle back on the scene. Electronic fuel injectors (EFI) were developed and replaced carburetors to feed air and fuel into the engine. These computerized controls help the engine to perform efficiently, while preventing the problem of engine knock. Electronic controls also help regulate toxic emissions.

(above right) The Ford Shelby Cobra GT500, created by car designer Carroll Shelby, made a comeback in 2006. It is considered the most powerful Mustang yet.

(below) The Dodge Charger was also redesigned for 2006. Two of the model's option packages feature the legendary Hemi V8 engine.

The Mustang Reloaded

The 2005 Ford Mustang was pure 1960s muscle. Its eye-catching design led a trend toward "retro" muscle cars, or cars that look and perform just like their original versions. In addition to the standard long hood, short deck, and short trunk, the new Mustang also featured a slightly hooded, black-colored grille and aggressive front-end shape of its earliest editions. The 2006 Mustang GT Premium retained the same shape and comes standard with a V8 engine, rear spoiler, and stainless steel dual exhaust.

The Future Unfolds

The rebirth of muscle dominated the 2006 auto shows, where car companies reveal new cars they might turn into full-production dealership models. One of the hottest **concept cars** was the restyled Dodge Challenger. The Challenger was styled to look like the original Challenger, but it included modern technology and accessories. Its most exciting feature was its legendary street Hemi engine, featuring 425 horsepower and a ton of torque.

(above) Ford introduced the Saleen Mustang in 2005. It features a high-performance V8 engine and superior handling capabilities.

(above) The Dodge Challenger appeared as a concept car at auto shows in 2006. Based on the 1970 model, the Challenger featured bold striping and an aggressive front grille.

The Hemi is Back!

The new Hemi V8 engine charged back onto the scene in 2003 under the hood of the Dodge Ram pickup truck. It featured a new design that allows it to use only four cylinders at cruising speeds instead of eight, which means it uses fuel more efficiently. The new Hemi was also included in the muscular Chrysler 300C, Dodge Magnum wagon, and the new Dodge Charger.

Leader of the Pack

Visions of speed and style drove the production of muscle cars, both on the street and on the track. Some individuals influenced the industry in significant ways. These people helped invent classic muscle cars and made them better through design and engineering.

Carroll Shelby

Carroll Shelby was a well-known automotive designer. In his early career, he was a successful race car driver. He won the famous 24-hour Le Mans race in France, and was named "Sports Car Driver of the Year" by Sports Illustrated magazine in both 1956 and 1957. His most famous automotive design was the Shelby-American AC Cobra of 1965. It is often considered to be one of the greatest American sports cars ever built because of its racing successes against Europe's best sports cars. Shelby designed special versions of the Mustang for racing, and they were highly regarded for their speed and style.

Shelby Stripes

The Shelby Mustang featured bold stripes across the car's hood. These stripes are now known as Shelby Stripes, and they are available as an option on most modern Mustangs today. These stripes can also be seen on some models of the Dodge Viper.

Carroll Shelby accepts a trophy after winning a race.

John DeLorean stands next to the DMC-12, which was featured as the time-traveling vehicle in the 1985 movie Back to the Future.

John DeLorean

John DeLorean was one of the driving forces behind Pontiac's GTO. DeLorean worked in the Pontiac division of General Motors for many years. There, he helped develop the GTO option package. After leaving General Motors, DeLorean founded his own company called the DeLorean Motor Company. The company made one model, a sports car called the DMC-12. It did not sell well and the company failed in less than five years. DeLorean died in 2005.

Tom Hoover

Tom Hoover is often referred to as the "Godfather of the Hemi." He was an engineer at Chrysler for almost 25 years, and developed some of racing's most powerful engines. His most famous contribution to the automotive world is the racing Hemi engine. Hoover adapted the Hemi for use in high-performance race cars. The engine dominated NASCAR racing until it was **banned** for not being a full-production engine, or an engine that came standard on regular production models. Hoover's Hemi is considered one of the most powerful engines ever developed.

Bill France waves from a race car window in 1939. France, or "Big Bill," was a mechanic and racing enthusiast. In 1948, he co-founded the National Association for Stock Car Auto Racing (NASCAR). Many muscle car designs were inspired by racing. Bill France died in 1992.

Glossary

aerodynamic A design that allows air to move over, under, and around a car better

ban To prohibit something

brand name The name of a business that is registered for exclusive use

carburetor A metal compartment where air and fuel are mixed together

chrome A shiny coating of the metal chromium

Clean Air Act A series of laws to improve air quality by reducing smog and air pollution

compress To squeeze something

concept car A model that a manufacturer is considering putting into regular production

confiscate To take something away

coupe A two-door car with a roof

cylinder A chamber in which a piston, or disc, pumps up and down

dealership A place where cars are purchased

disc brakes Pads that stop a vehicle by applying pressure to a disc that sits next to a wheel

division A small company within a larger one

embargo A ban on trade with a specific country

fiberglass A material made of fine strands of glass

fine To make someone pay an amount of money

grille Metal grates at the front of a car that allow air under the hood to cool the engine

hardtop A roof made of a hard, solid material

Middle East An area of northern Africa and southwestern Asia

modify To change something

Plexiglas Light, see-through plastic

restore To make something like the original

shock absorbers Springs that cushion a car from bumps in the road

spokespeople People who represent a cause, such as road safety

sport suspension A stiff, sturdy set of springs and shock absorbers that help a car handle bumps in the road

torque A force that relates to how much power an engine can produce

toxic emissions Poisonous gases that are released from an engine

upgrade To make something better or worth more

Index

Printed in the U.S.A.